SORRY, WRONG NUMBER and THE HITCH-HIKER

BY LUCILLE FLETCHER

★

★

DRAMATISTS
PLAY SERVICE
INC.

SPECIAL NOTE

PREFACE TO "SORRY, WRONG NUMBER"

This play was originally designed as an experiment in sound and not just as a murder story, with the telephone as its chief protagonist. I wanted to write something that by its very nature should, for maximum effectiveness, be heard rather than seen. However, in the hands of a fine actress like Agnes Moorhead, the script turned out to be more the character study of a woman than a technical experiment, and the plot itself, with its O. Henry twist at the end, fell into the thriller category. Hence it became more than I had originally intended, finding (as sometimes happens with brain-children) wider horizons than I had imagined for it. It has, since its birth in radio, been done also on television, on the stage as a one-act play, and finally, in expanded form, as a movie with Barbara Stanwyck playing the role of Mrs. Stevenson. The text as it appears in this volume is the original radio version, as acted by Miss Moorhead many times on *Suspense*. It is still, as I see it, a simple tale of horror, depending for its merits to a great extent on the device of the telephone. The busy signal, the crossed wires, the mechanical voices of the operators, are its chief technical elements, providing the conflict without which Mrs. Stevenson's dilemma would be impossible. It is still what we do *not* see but merely guess at, even in her speeches, the overtones of querulousness, and the hints of her life she lets drop, that give the script its mood of mounting horror.

In order to read or produce this play in its original radio version, the director should clearly understand that the radio version should *not* include those stage directions and speeches which are now enclosed between brackets ([]). The additions to the original version now between brackets are intended for the use of groups wishing to produce the play on a platform, and simulating an actual radio broadcast in a studio. When the play is done this way, Mrs. Stevenson may be shown in bed, with three flats assumed to be separating her room from the rest of the stage, and the other actors and members of the crew spotlighted in the outer periphery of darkness. Costumes, telephone, props, even the *slight* suggestion of a main set might be added, though this last is certainly not necessary. The play has been used in this way and with great success on television, and (as a play on the stage) by the Pittsburgh Playhouse. In such a version, of course, many of the smaller telephone sound effects may be omitted entirely. I suggest only the actual ringing through of the phone calls. The other phone sounds might easily be indicated by the gestures and facial expression of the actress who plays Mrs. Stevenson. Indeed, this type of performance would concentrate more on the appearance and character of the actress and somewhat less on external effects, thus making it a dramatic portrait of loneliness and terror surrounded, as it were, and trapped within four walls. If the play is produced in the way first above described, I suggest that the lighting of the main set be fairly low, perhaps only a lamp near Mrs. Stevenson's bed. This lamp, which in the last scene she overthrows in her terror, would of course bring to an effective black-out finish the actual murder.

There is also another effective method of presenting the play. A somewhat closer approximation to the effect produced over the radio may be secured if the radio version (the version, that is, that makes *no* use of the stage directions and dialogue between brackets) is played exactly as written. However, this method requires that the play should be produced in darkness. The production in that event would probably be most effectively made in a studio or other room behind the scenes in an actual auditorium and allowed to make its effect either direct upon the audience attending, or it could be actually broadcast over a *local* public address loudspeaker. Only in this way can the *machinery* of the telephone be heard—the small, irritating signals which give our heroine her first premonition of disaster, and inevitably lead her on through frustration, hysteria and desperation to her final doom. Through the mere fact of their invisibility, the characters Mrs. Stevenson speaks to become more frightening, and more exasperating. The murder itself, heard only as chaotic sound over a telephone wire, is more effective, and it seems to me more moving, than when seen in full view on a stage.

All sound effects, as indicated either in the radio or the expanded version, are extremely simple, and involve almost without exception various uses of the telephone. It would probably add to the over-all effect of the production if real telephone equipment were used, though if this is not readily available it is suggested that a toy phone could reproduce the sound of dialing. The director will also not find it particularly difficult to devise means of reproducing the necessary sounds of dialing, buzzers, and the like. The sound of the train offstage will probably have to be reproduced by a sound effects record. Dramatists Play Service can furnish this record (No. 5049), price, $3.75, which includes packing and shipping charges.

No music has ever been used with this script; music of any kind would serve only to detract from its reality.

Aside from its emphasis on mechanics, this play requires acting above all, not only by the woman who plays Mrs. Stevenson (who should not in any event overplay the role), but by every subordinate player, brief though his bit may be. Each should present a little vignette of human nature, and we should feel that the people we are hearing are real operators, a real policeman, a real gangster, etc. Each operator, though speaking ordinary lines, should stand out as a distinct type, both physically and vocally. It is life itself which Mrs. Stevenson strives so frantically to make contact with over her telephone, and we must believe for the moment in its reality, its variety, its calm matter-of-factness, and its indifference. Only by doing this will her lonely, neurotic personality be outlined for the empty thing it is.

One final word. Though I have gladly consented to provide a script which can be produced in more ways than one, and I believe that producing groups interested both in the "straight" theatre and in radio production will find something of interest, as well as a challenge in the mere mechanics of the production, it is only natural that as author I believe that the original radio version, as it was done so often over the radio, still offers the most effective means by which it can be produced. However, I regard the invitation extended to me to provide a different means of production as a distinct challenge, and I shall be interested to learn how the alternative versions just mentioned succeed with the public.

LUCILLE FLETCHER

CAST

MRS. STEVENSON
1ST OPERATOR
1ST MAN
2ND MAN
CHIEF OPERATOR
2ND OPERATOR
3RD OPERATOR
4TH OPERATOR
5TH OPERATOR
INFORMATION
HOSPITAL RECEPTIONIST
WESTERN UNION
SERGEANT DUFFY
A LUNCH ROOM COUNTER ATTENDANT *

TECHNICAL STAFF

DIRECTOR
SOUND EFFECTS MAN
STAGE MANAGER *

NOTE: The suggested additions for a visual presentation of this play are to be found within brackets, and are indicated by the word, "Scene" before each addition. If the play is to be done invisibly, over a P. A. loudspeaker system, pay no attention to the parentheses. Without them, one has the original radio version.

* Added for visual presentation.

Sorry, Wrong Number

[SCENE: *As curtain rises, we see a divided stage, only the center part of which is lighted and furnished as* MRS. STEVENSON'S *bedroom. Expensive, rather fussy furnishings. A large bed, on which* MRS. STEVENSON, *clad in bed-jacket, is lying. A night-table close by, with phone, lighted lamp, and pill bottles. A mantel, with clock,* R. *A closed door,* R. *A window, with curtains closed, rear. The set is lit by one lamp on night-table. It is enclosed by three flats. Beyond this central set, the stage, on either side, is in darkness.*
MRS. STEVENSON *is dialling a number on phone, as curtain rises. She listens to phone, slams down receiver in irritation. As she does so, we hear sound of a train roaring by in the distance. She reaches for her pill bottle, pours herself a glass of water, shakes out pill, swallows it, then reaches for phone again, dials number nervously.*] SOUND: *Number being dialled on phone: Busy signal.*

MRS. STEVENSON. (*A querulous, self-centered neurotic.*) Oh—*dear!* (*Slams down receiver. Dials* OPERATOR.) [SCENE: *A spotlight,* L. *of side flat, picks up out of peripheral darkness, figure of* 1ST OPERATOR, *sitting with headphones at small table. If spotlight not available, use flashlight, clicked on by* 1ST OPERATOR, *illumining her face.*]
OPERATOR. Your call, please?
MRS. STEVENSON. Operator? I've been dialling Murray Hill 4-0098 now for the last three-quarters of an hour, and the line is always busy. But I don't see how it *could* be busy that long. Will you try it for me, please?
OPERATOR. Murray Hill 4-0098? One moment, please. [SCENE: *She makes gesture of plugging in call through a switchboard.*]
MRS. STEVENSON. I don't see how it could be busy all this time. It's my husband's office. He's working late tonight, and I'm all

alone here in the house. My health is very poor—and I've been feeling so nervous all day. . . .

OPERATOR. Ringing Murray Hill 4-0098. . . . (SOUND: *Phone buzz. It rings three times. Receiver is picked up at other end.*) [SCENE: *Spotlight picks up figure of a heavy-set man, seated at desk with phone on* R. *side of dark periphery of stage. He is wearing a hat. Picks up phone, which rings three times.*]

MAN. Hello.

MRS. STEVENSON. Hello . . . ? (*A little puzzled.*) Hello. Is Mr. Stevenson there?

MAN. (*Into phone, as though he had not heard.*) Hello. . . . (*Louder.*) Hello. [SCENE: *Spotlight on* L. *now moves from* OPERATOR *to another man,* GEORGE. *A killer type, also wearing hat, but standing as in a phone booth. A three-sided screen may be used to suggest this.*]

2ND MAN. (*Slow heavy quality, faintly foreign accent.*) Hello.

1ST MAN. Hello. George?

GEORGE. Yes, sir.

MRS. STEVENSON. (*Louder and more imperious, to phone.*) Hello. Who's this? What number am I calling, please?

1ST MAN. We have heard from our client. He says the coast is clear for tonight.

GEORGE. Yes, sir.

1ST MAN. Where are you now?

GEORGE. In a phone booth.

1ST MAN. Okay. You know the address. At eleven o'clock the private patrolman goes around to the bar on Second Avenue for a beer. Be sure that all the lights downstairs are out. There should be only one light visible from the street. At eleven-fifteen a subway train crosses the bridge. It makes a noise in case her window is open, and she should scream.

MRS. STEVENSON. (*Shocked.*) Oh—HELLO! What number is this, please?

GEORGE. Okay. I understand.

1ST MAN. Make it quick. As little blood as possible. Our client does not wish to make her suffer long.

GEORGE. A knife okay, sir?

1ST MAN. Yes. A knife will be okay. And remember—remove the rings and bracelets, and the jewelry in the bureau drawer. Our client wishes it to look like simple robbery.

GEORGE. Okay—I get —— [SCENE: *Spotlight suddenly goes out on* GEORGE.] (SOUND: *A bland buzzing signal.*) [SCENE: *Spotlight goes off on* 1ST MAN.]

MRS. STEVENSON. (*Clicking phone.*) Oh . . . ! (*Bland buzzing signal continues. She hangs up.*) How awful! How unspeakably . . . [SCENE: *She lies back on her pillows, overcome for a few seconds, then suddenly pulls herself together, reaches for phone.*] (SOUND: *Dialling. Phone buzz.*) [SCENE: *Spotlight goes on at* 1ST OPERATOR'S *switchboard.* 1ST *and* 2ND MAN *exit as unobtrusively as possible, in darkness.*]

OPERATOR. Your call, please?

MRS. STEVENSON. (*Unnerved and breathless, into phone.*) Operator. I—I've just been cut off.

OPERATOR. I'm sorry, madam. What number were you calling?

MRS. STEVENSON. Why—it was supposed to be Murray Hill 4-0098, but it wasn't. Some wires must have crossed—I was cut into a wrong number—and—I've just heard the most dreadful thing—a—a murder—and—(*Imperiously.*) Operator, you'll simply have to retrace that call at once.

OPERATOR. I beg your pardon, madam—I don't quite ——

MRS. STEVENSON. Oh—I know it was a wrong number, and I had no business listening—but these two men—they were cold-blooded fiends—and they were going to murder somebody—some poor innocent woman—who was all alone—in a house near a bridge. And we've got to stop them—we've got to ——

OPERATOR. (*Patiently.*) What number were you calling, madam?

MRS. STEVENSON. That doesn't matter. This was a *wrong* number. And *you* dialled it. And we've got to find out what it was —immediately!

OPERATOR. But—madam ——

MRS. STEVENSON. Oh—why are you so stupid? Look—it was obviously a case of some little slip of the finger. I told you to try Murray Hill 4-0098 for me—you dialed it—but your finger must have slipped—and I was connected with some other number—and I could hear them, but they couldn't hear me. Now, I simply fail to see why you couldn't make that same mistake again—on purpose—why you couldn't *try* to dial Murray Hill 4-0098 in the same careless sort of way. . . .

OPERATOR. (*Quickly.*) Murray Hill 4-0098? I will try to get it for you, madam.

MRS. STEVENSON. (*Sarcastically.*) *Thank* you. [SCENE: *She bridles, adjusts herself on her pillows, reaches for handkerchief, wipes forehead, glancing uneasily for a moment toward window, while still holding phone.*] (*Sound of ringing: Busy signal.*)

OPERATOR. I am sorry. Murray Hill 4-0098 is busy.

MRS. STEVENSON. (*Frantically clicking receiver.*) Operator. Operator.

OPERATOR. Yes, madam.

MRS. STEVENSON. (*Angrily.*) You *didn't* try to get that wrong number at all. I asked explicitly. And all you did was dial correctly.

OPERATOR. I am sorry. What number were you calling?

MRS. STEVENSON. Can't you, for once, forget what number I was calling, and do something specific? Now I want to trace that call. It's my civic duty—it's *your* civic duty—to trace that call . . . and to apprehend those dangerous killers—and if *you* won't . . .

OPERATOR. (*Glancing around wearily.*) I will connect you with the Chief Operator.

MRS. STEVENSON. *Please!* (*Sound of ringing.*) [SCENE: OPERATOR *puts hand over mouthpiece of phone, gestures into darkness. A half whisper:*

[OPERATOR. Miss Curtis. Will you pick up on 17, please? (MISS CURTIS, *Chief Operator, enters. Middle-aged, efficient type, pleasant. Wearing headphones.*)

MISS CURTIS. Yes, dear. What's the trouble?

OPERATOR. Somebody wanting a call traced. I can't make head nor tail of it. . . .

MISS CURTIS. (*Sitting down at desk, as* OPERATOR *gets up.*) Sure, dear. 17? (*She makes gesture of plugging in her headphone.*)]

CHIEF OPERATOR. (*Coolly and professionally.*) This is the Chief Operator.

MRS. STEVENSON. Chief Operator? I want you to trace a call. A telephone call. Immediately. I don't know where it came from, or who was making it, but it's absolutely necessary that it be tracked down. Because it was about a murder. Yes, a terrible, cold-blooded murder of a poor innocent woman—tonight at eleven-fifteen.

CHIEF OPERATOR. I see.

MRS. STEVENSON. (*High-strung, demanding.*) Can you trace it for me? Can you track down those men?

CHIEF OPERATOR. It depends, madam.

MRS. STEVENSON. Depends on what?

CHIEF OPERATOR. It depends on whether the call is still going on. If it's a live call, we can trace it on the equipment. If it's been disconnected, we can't.

MRS. STEVENSON. Disconnected?

CHIEF OPERATOR. If the parties have stopped talking to each other.

MRS. STEVENSON. Oh—but—but of course they must have stopped talking to each other by *now*. That was at least five minutes ago—and they didn't sound like the type who would make a long call.

CHIEF OPERATOR. Well, I can try tracing it. [SCENE: *She takes pencil out of her hair-do.*] Now—what is your name, madam?

MRS. STEVENSON. Mrs. Stevenson. Mrs. Elbert Stevenson. But —listen ——

CHIEF OPERATOR. (*Writing it down.*) And your telephone number?

MRS. STEVENSON. (*More irritated.*) Plaza 4-2295. But if you go on wasting all this time —— [SCENE: *She glances at clock on mantel.*]

CHIEF OPERATOR. And what is your reason for wanting this call traced?

MRS. STEVENSON. My reason? Well—for Heaven's sake—isn't it obvious? I overhear two men—they're killers—they're planning to murder this woman—it's a matter for the police.

CHIEF OPERATOR. Have you told the police?

MRS. STEVENSON. No. How could I?

CHIEF OPERATOR. You're making this check into a private call purely as a private individual?

MRS. STEVENSON. Yes. But meanwhile ——

CHIEF OPERATOR. Well, Mrs. Stevenson—I seriously doubt whether we could make this check for you at this time just on your say-so as a private individual. We'd have to have something more official.

MRS. STEVENSON. Oh—for Heaven's sake! You mean to tell me I can't report a murder without getting tied up in all this red-tape? Why—it's perfectly idiotic. All right, then. I *will* call the police. (*She slams down receiver.*) [SCENE: *Spotlight goes off on two* OPERATORS.] Ridiculous! (*Sound of dialling.*) [SCENE: MRS. STEVENSON *dials number on phone, as two* OPERATORS *exit unobtrusively in darkness.*] (*On* R. *of stage, spotlight picks up a* 2ND OPERATOR, *seated like first, with headphones at table* [*same one vacated by* 1ST MAN].)
2ND OPERATOR. Your call, please?
MRS. STEVENSON. (*Very annoyed.*) The Police Department—*please.*
2ND OPERATOR. Ringing the Police Department. (*Ring twice. Phone is picked up.*) [SCENE: L. *stage, at table vacated by* 1ST *and* CHIEF OPERATOR, *spotlight now picks up* SERGEANT DUFFY, *seated in a relaxed position. Just entering beside him is a young man in cap and apron, carrying a large brown paper parcel, delivery boy for a local lunch counter. Phone is ringing.*
YOUNG MAN. Here's your lunch, Sarge. They didn't have no jelly doughnuts, so I give you French crullers. Okay, Sarge?
S. DUFFY. French crullers. I got ulcers. Whyn't you make it apple pie? (*Picks up phone, which has rung twice.*)] Police Department. Precinct 43. Duffy speaking.
[SCENE: LUNCH ROOM ATTENDANT. (*Anxiously.*) We don't have no apple pie, either, Sarge ——]
MRS. STEVENSON. Police Department? Oh. This is Mrs. Stevenson—Mrs. Elbert Smythe Stevenson of 53 North Sutton Place. I'm calling up to report a murder. [SCENE: DUFFY *has been examining lunch, but double-takes suddenly on above.*]
DUFFY. Eh?
MRS. STEVENSON. I mean—the murder hasn't been committed yet. I just overheard plans for it over the telephone . . . over a wrong number that the operator gave me. [SCENE: DUFFY *relaxes, sighs, starts taking lunch from bag.*] I've been trying to trace down the call myself, but everybody is so stupid—and I guess in the end you're the only people who could *do* anything.
DUFFY. (*Not too impressed.*) [SCENE: *Pays* ATTENDANT, *who exits.*] Yes, ma'am.
MRS. STEVENSON. (*Trying to impress him.*) It was a perfectly

definite murder. I heard their plans distinctly. [SCENE: DUFFY *begins to eat sandwich, phone at his ear.*] Two men were talking, and they were going to murder some woman at eleven-fifteen tonight—she lived in a house near a bridge.

DUFFY. Yes, ma'am.

MRS. STEVENSON. And there was a private patrolman on the street. He was going to go around for a beer on Second Avenue. And there was some third man—a client, who was paying to have this poor woman murdered—they were going to take her rings and bracelets—and use a knife . . . well, it's unnerved me dreadfully—and I'm not well. . . .

DUFFY. I see. [SCENE: *Having finished sandwich, he wipes mouth with paper napkin.*] When was all this, ma'am?

MRS. STEVENSON. About eight minutes ago. Oh . . . (*Relieved.*) then you *can* do something? You *do* understand——

DUFFY. And what is your name, ma'am? [SCENE: *He reaches for pad.*]

MRS. STEVENSON. (*Impatiently.*) Mrs. Stevenson. Mrs. Elbert Stevenson.

DUFFY. And your address?

MRS. STEVENSON. 53 North Sutton Place. *That's* near a bridge. The Queensboro Bridge, you know—and *we* have a private patrolman on *our* street—and Second Avenue——

DUFFY. And what was that number you were calling?

MRS. STEVENSON. Murray Hill 4-0098. [SCENE: DUFFY *writes it down.*] But—that wasn't the number I overheard. I mean Murray Hill 4-0098 is my husband's office. [SCENE: DUFFY, *in exasperation, holds pencil poised.*] He's working late tonight, and I was trying to reach him to ask him to come home. I'm an invalid, you know—and it's the maid's night off—and I *hate* to be alone—even though he says I'm perfectly safe as long as I have the telephone right beside my bed.

DUFFY. (*Stolidly.*) [SCENE: *He has put pencil down, pushes pad away.*] Well—we'll look into it, Mrs. Stevenson—and see if we can check it with the telephone company.

MRS. STEVENSON. (*Getting impatient.*) But the telephone company said they couldn't check the call if the parties had stopped talking. I've already taken care of *that.*

DUFFY. Oh—yes? [SCENE: *He yawns slightly.*]

MRS. STEVENSON. (*High-handed.*) Personally I feel you ought to do something far more immediate and drastic than just check the call. What good does checking the call do, if they've stopped talking? By the time you track it down, they'll already have committed the murder.

DUFFY. [SCENE: *He reaches for paper cup of coffee.*] Well—we'll take care of it, lady. Don't worry. [SCENE: *He begins to take off paper top of coffee container.*]

MRS. STEVENSON. I'd say the whole thing calls for a search—a complete and thorough search of the whole city. [SCENE: DUFFY *puts down phone for a moment, to work on cap, as her voice continues.*] I'm very near a bridge, and I'm not far from Second Avenue. And I know *I'd* feel a whole lot better if you sent around a radio car to *this* neighborhood at once.

DUFFY. [SCENE: *Picks up phone again, drinks coffee.*] And what makes you think the murder's gcing to be committed in your neighborhood, ma'am?

MRS. STEVENSON. Oh—I don't know. The coincidence is so horrible. Second Avenue—the patrolman—the bridge . . .

DUFFY. [SCENE: *He sips coffee.*] Second Avenue is a very long street, ma'am. And do you happen to know how many bridges there are in the city of New York alone? Not to mention Brooklyn, Staten Island, Queens, and the Bronx? And how do you know there isn't some little house out on Staten Island—on some little Second Avenue you've never heard about? [SCENE: *A long gulp of coffee.*] How do you know they were even talking about New York at all?

MRS. STEVENSON. But I heard the call on the New York dialling system.

DUFFY. How do you know it wasn't a long distance call you overheard? Telephones are funny things. [SCENE: *He sets down coffee.*] Look, lady, why don't you look at it this way? Supposing you hadn't broken in on that telephone call? Supposing you'd got your husband the way you always do? Would this murder have made any difference to you then?

MRS. STEVENSON. I suppose not. But it's so inhuman—so cold-blooded . . .

DUFFY. A lot of murders are committed in this city every day, ma'am. If we could do something to stop 'em, we would. But a clue of this kind that's so vague isn't much more use to us than no clue at all.

MRS. STEVENSON. But, surely ——

DUFFY. Unless, of course, you have some reason for thinking this call is phony—and that someone may be planning to murder *you?*

MRS. STEVENSON. *Me?* Oh—no—I hardly think so. I—I mean—why should anybody? I'm alone all day and night—I see nobody except my maid Eloise—she's a big two-hundred-pounder—she's too lazy to bring up my breakfast tray—and the only other person is my husband Elbert—he's crazy about me—adores me—waits on me hand and foot—he's scarcely left my side since I took sick twelve years ago ——

DUFFY. Well—then—there's nothing for you to worry about, is there? [SCENE: LUNCH COUNTER ATTENDANT *has entered. He is carrying a piece of apple pie on a plate. Points it out to* DUFFY *triumphantly.*] And now—if you'll just leave the rest of this to us ——

MRS. STEVENSON. But what will you *do?* It's so late—it's nearly eleven o'clock.

DUFFY. (*Firmly.*) [SCENE: *He nods to* ATTENDANT, *pleased.*] We'll take care of it, lady.

MRS. STEVENSON. Will you broadcast it all over the city? And send out squads? And warn your radio cars to watch out—especially in suspicious neighborhoods like mine? [SCENE: ATTENDANT, *in triumph, has put pie down in front of* DUFFY. *Takes fork out of his pocket, stands at attention, waiting.*]

DUFFY. (*More firmly.*) Lady, I *said* we'd take care of it. [SCENE: *Glances at pie.*] Just now I've got a couple of other matters here on my desk that require my immediate ——

MRS. STEVENSON. Oh! (*She slams down receiver hard.*) Idiot. [SCENE: DUFFY, *listening at phone, hangs up. Shrugs. Winks at* ATTENDANT *as though to say, "What a crazy character!" Attacks his pie as spotlight on him fades out.*] (MRS. STEVENSON, *in bed, looking at phone nervously.*) Now—why did I do that? Now—he'll think I *am* a fool. [SCENE: *She sits there tensely, then throws herself back against pillows, lies there a moment, whimpering with self-pity.*] Oh—why doesn't Elbert come home? *Why* doesn't he? [SCENE: *We hear sound of train roaring by in the distance. She sits up reaching for phone.*] (*Sound of dialling operator.*) [SCENE: *Spotlight picks up* 2ND OPERATOR, *seated* R.]

OPERATOR. Your call, please?

MRS. STEVENSON. Operator—for Heaven's sake—will you ring that Murray Hill 4-0098 number again? I can't think what's keeping him so long.

OPERATOR. Ringing Murray Hill 4-0098. (*Rings. Busy signal.*) The line is busy. Shall I ——

MRS. STEVENSON. (*Nastily.*) I can hear it. You don't have to tell me. I know it's busy. (*Slams down receiver.*) [SCENE: *Spotlight fades off on* 2ND OPERATOR.] [SCENE: MRS. STEVENSON *sinks back against pillows again, whimpering to herself fretfully. She glances at clock, then turning, punches her pillows up, trying to make herself comfortable. But she isn't. Whimpers to herself as she squirms restlessly in bed.*] If I could only get out of this bed for a little while. If I could get a breath of fresh air—or just lean out the window—and see the street. . . . [SCENE: *She sighs, reaches for pill bottle, shakes out a pill. As she does so:*] (*The phone rings. She darts for it instantly.*) Hello. Elbert? Hello. Hello. Hello. Oh—what's the *matter* with this phone? HELLO? HELLO? (*Slams down receiver.*) [SCENE: *She stares at it, tensely.*] (*The phone rings again. Once. She picks it up.*) Hello? Hello. . . . Oh—for Heaven's sake—who *is* this? Hello. Hello. HELLO. (*Slams down receiver. Dials operator.*) [SCENE: *Spotlight comes on* L., *showing* 3RD OPERATOR, *at spot vacated by* DUFFY.]

3RD OPERATOR. Your call, please?

MRS. STEVENSON. (*Very annoyed and imperious.*) Hello. Operator. I don't know what's the matter with this telephone tonight, but it's positively driving me crazy. I've never seen such inefficient, miserable service. Now, look. I'm an invalid, and I'm very nervous, and I'm *not* supposed to be annoyed. But if this keeps on much longer . . .

3RD OPERATOR. (*A young sweet type.*) What seems to be the trouble, madam?

MRS. STEVENSON. Well—everything's wrong. The whole world could be murdered, for all you people care. And now—my phone keeps ringing. . . .

OPERATOR. Yes, madam?

MRS. STEVENSON. Ringing and ringing and ringing every five seconds or so, and when I pick it up, there's no one there.

OPERATOR. I am sorry, madam. If you will hang up, I will test it for you.
MRS. STEVENSON. I don't want you to test it for me. I want you to put through that call—whatever it is—at once.
OPERATOR. (*Gently.*) I am afraid that is not possible, madam.
MRS. STEVENSON. (*Storming.*) Not possible? And why—may I ask?
OPERATOR. The system is automatic, madam. If someone is trying to dial your number, there is no way to check whether the call is coming through the system or not—unless the person who is trying to reach you complains to his particular operator ——
MRS. STEVENSON. Well, of all the stupid, complicated . . . ! And meanwhile *I've* got to sit here in my bed, *suffering* every time that phone rings—imagining everything. . . .
OPERATOR. I will try to check it for you, madam.
MRS. STEVENSON. Check it! Check it! That's all anybody can do. Of all the stupid, idiotic . . . ! (*She hangs up.*) Oh—what's the use . . . [SCENE: 3RD OPERATOR *fades out of spotlight, as*] (*Instantly* MRS. STEVENSON'S *phone rings again. She picks up receiver. Wildly.*) Hello. HELLO. Stop ringing, do you hear me? Answer me? What do you want? Do you realize you're driving me crazy? [SCENE: *Spotlight goes on* R. *We see a* MAN *in eye-shade and shirt-sleeves, at desk with phone and telegrams.*] Stark, staring . . .
MAN. (*Dull flat voice.*) Hello. Is this Plaza 4-2295?
MRS. STEVENSON. (*Catching her breath.*) Yes. Yes. This is Plaza 4-2295.
WESTERN UNION. This is Western Union. I have a telegram here for Mrs. Elbert Stevenson. Is there anyone there to receive the message?
MRS. STEVENSON. (*Trying to calm herself.*) I am Mrs. Stevenson.
WESTERN UNION. (*Reading flatly.*) The telegram is as follows: "Mrs. Elbert Stevenson. 53 North Sutton Place, New York, New York. Darling. Terribly sorry. Tried to get you for last hour, but line busy. Leaving for Boston eleven p. m. tonight on urgent business. Back tomorrow afternoon. Keep happy. Love. Signed. Elbert."

MRS. STEVENSON. (*Breathlessly, aghast, to herself.*) Oh . . . no . . .

WESTERN UNION. That is all, madam. Do you wish us to deliver a copy of the message?

MRS. STEVENSON. No—no, thank you.

WESTERN UNION. Thank you, madam. Good night. (*He hangs up phone.*) [SCENE: *Spotlight on* WESTERN UNION *immediately out.*]

MRS. STEVENSON. (*Mechanically, to phone.*) Good night. (*She hangs up slowly. Suddenly bursting into.*) No—no—it isn't true! He couldn't do it! Not when he knows I'll be all alone. It's some trick—some fiendish . . . [SCENE: *We hear sound of train roaring by outside. She half rises in bed, in panic, glaring toward curtains. Her movements are frenzied. She beats with her knuckles on bed, then suddenly stops, and reaches for phone.*] (*She dials operator.*) [SCENE: *Spotlight picks up* 4TH OPERATOR, *seated* L.]

OPERATOR. (*Coolly.*) Your call, please?

MRS. STEVENSON. Operator—try that Murray Hill 4-0098 number for me just once more, please.

OPERATOR. Ringing Murray Hill 4-0098. (*Call goes through. We hear ringing at other end. Ring after ring.*) [SCENE: *If telephone noises are not used visually, have* OPERATOR *say after a brief pause: " They do not answer."*]

MRS. STEVENSON. He's gone. Oh—Elbert, how could you? How could you . . . ? (*She hangs up phone, sobbing pityingly to herself, turning restlessly.*) [SCENE: *Spotlight goes out on* 4TH OPERATOR.] But I can't be alone tonight. I can't. If I'm alone one more second . . . [SCENE: *She runs hands wildly through hair.*] I don't care what he says—or what the expense is—I'm a sick woman—I'm entitled . . . [SCENE: *With trembling fingers she picks up receiver again.*] (*She dials* INFORMATION.) [SCENE: *The spotlight picks up* INFORMATION OPERATOR, *seated* R.]

INFORMATION. This is Information.

MRS. STEVENSON. I want the telephone number of Henchley Hospital.

INFORMATION. Henchley Hospital? Do you have the address, madam?

MRS. STEVENSON. No. It's somewhere in the 70's, though. It's a very small, private and exclusive hospital where I had my appendix out two years ago. Henchley. H-E-N-C ——

INFORMATION. One moment, please.

MRS. STEVENSON. Please—hurry. And please—what *is* the time?

INFORMATION. I do not know, madam. You may find out the time by dialling Meridian 7-1212.

MRS. STEVENSON. (*Irritated.*) Oh—for Heaven's sake! Couldn't you ——?

INFORMATION. The number of Henchley Hospital is Butterfield 7-0105, madam.

MRS. STEVENSON. Butterfield 7-0105. (*She hangs up before she finishes speaking, and immediately dials number as she repeats it.*) [SCENE: *Spotlight goes out on* INFORMATION.] (*Phone rings.*) [SCENE: *Spotlight picks up a* WOMAN *in nurse's uniform, seated at desk,* L.]

WOMAN. (*Middle-aged, solid, firm, practical.*) Henchley Hospital, good evening.

MRS. STEVENSON. Nurses' Registry.

WOMAN. Who was it you wished to speak to, please?

MRS. STEVENSON. (*High-handed.*) I want the Nurses' Registry at once. I want a trained nurse. I want to hire her immediately. For the night.

WOMAN. I see. And what is the nature of the case, madam?

MRS. STEVENSON. Nerves. I'm very nervous. I need soothing—and companionship. My husband is away—and I'm ——

WOMAN. Have you been recommended to us by any doctor in particular, madam?

MRS. STEVENSON. No. But I really don't see why all this catechizing is necessary. I want a trained nurse. I was a patient in your hospital two years ago. And after all, I *do* expect to *pay* this person ——

WOMAN. We quite understand that, madam. But registered nurses are very scarce just now—and our superintendent has asked us to send people out only on cases where the physician in charge feels it is absolutely necessary.

MRS. STEVENSON. (*Growing hysterical.*) Well—it *is* absolutely necessary. I'm a sick woman. I—I'm very upset. Very. I'm alone in this house—and I'm an invalid—and tonight I overheard a telephone conversation that upset me dreadfully. About a murder—a poor woman who was going to be murdered at eleven-fifteen tonight—in fact, if someone doesn't come at once —I'm afraid I'll go out of my mind. . . . (*Almost off handle by now.*)

WOMAN. (*Calmly.*) I see. Well—I'll speak to Miss Phillips as soon as she comes in. And what is your name, madam?

MRS. STEVENSON. Miss Phillips. And when do you expect her in?

WOMAN. I really don't know, madam. She went out to supper at eleven o'clock.

MRS. STEVENSON. Eleven o'clock. But it's not eleven yet. (*She cries out.*) Oh, my clock *has* stopped. I thought it was running down. What time is it? [SCENE: WOMAN *glances at wrist-watch.*]

WOMAN. Just fourteen minutes past eleven. . . . (*Sound of phone receiver being lifted on same line as* MRS. STEVENSON'S. *A click.*)

MRS. STEVENSON. (*Crying out.*) What's *that?*

WOMAN. What was what, madam?

MRS. STEVENSON. That—that click just now—in my own telephone? As though someone had lifted the receiver off the hook of the extension phone downstairs. . . .

WOMAN. I didn't hear it, madam. Now—about this . . .

MRS. STEVENSON. (*Scared.*) But I *did.* There's someone in this house. Someone downstairs in the kitchen. And they're listening to me now. They're . . . [SCENE: *She puts hand over her mouth.*] (*Hangs up phone.*) [SCENE: *She sits there, in terror, frozen, listening.*] (*In a suffocated voice.*) I won't pick it up. I won't let them hear me. I'll be quiet—and they'll think . . . (*With growing terror.*) But if I don't call someone now—while they're still down there—there'll be no time. . . . (*She picks up receiver. Bland buzzing signal. She dials operator. Ring twice.*) [SCENE: *On second ring, spotlight goes on* R. *We see* 5TH OPERATOR.]

OPERATOR. (*Fat and lethargic.*) Your call, please?

MRS. STEVENSON. (*A desperate whisper.*) Operator—I—I'm in desperate trouble . . . I ——

OPERATOR. I cannot hear you, madam. Please speak louder.

MRS. STEVENSON. (*Still whispering.*) I don't dare. I—there's someone listening. Can you hear me now?

OPERATOR. Your call, please? What number are you calling, madam?

MRS. STEVENSON. (*Desperately.*) You've got to hear me. Oh—please. You've got to help me. There's someone in this house. Someone who's going to murder me. And you've got to get in touch with the . . . (*Click of receiver being put down in* MRS. STEVENSON'S *line. Bursting out wildly.*) Oh—there it is . . . he's put it down . . . he's put down the extension . . . he's coming . . . (*She screams.*) he's coming up the stairs. . . . [SCENE: *She thrashes in bed, phone cord catching in lamp wire, lamp topples, goes out. Darkness.*] (*Hoarsely.*) Give me the Police Department. . . . [SCENE: *We see on the dark* C. *stage, the shadow of door opening.*] (*Screaming.*) The police! . . . [SCENE: *On stage, swift rush of a shadow, advancing to bed—sound of her voice is choked out, as*]

OPERATOR. Ringing the Police Department. (*Phone is rung. We hear sound of a train beginning to fade in. On second ring,* MRS. STEVENSON *screams again, but roaring of train drowns out her voice. For a few seconds we hear nothing but roaring of train, then dying away, phone at police headquarters ringing.*) [SCENE: *Spotlight goes on* DUFFY, L. *stage.*]

DUFFY. Police Department. Precinct 43. Duffy speaking. (*Pause.*) [SCENE: *Nothing visible but darkness on* C. *stage.*] Police Department. Duffy speaking. [SCENE: *A flashlight goes on, illuminating open phone to one side of* MRS. STEVENSON'S *bed. Nearby, hanging down, is her lifeless hand. We see the second man,* GEORGE, *in black gloves, reach down and pick up phone. He is breathing hard.*]

GEORGE. Sorry. Wrong number. (*Hangs up.*) [SCENE: *He replaces receiver on hook quietly, exits, as* DUFFY *hangs up with a shrug, and CURTAIN FALLS.*]

THE END

PREFACE TO "THE HITCH-HIKER"

THE HITCH-HIKER was written for Orson Welles in the days when he was one of the master producers and actors in radio. It was designed to provide a vehicle not only for his famous voice, but for the original techniques of sound which became associated with his radio productions.

Its production therefore provides two challenges: first for the star himself, who may regard it as an instrument of dramatic virtuosity; second, for the corps of assisting players and the sound crew, without whom its constantly changing scenery and eerie episodes would lose much of their effectiveness. As a production it must, in every sense of the word, be cooperative, down to the last " Halloo " from the Hitch-Hiker, to the last dropping of the last coin into the telephone.

It was written originally as a radio play. Its effect depends largely on the imaginative values as conveyed through the ear, rather than the eye. However, the present text is so arranged that it may be used by " live " actors on the stage, and as such it may be done in one of two ways: (1) Actually shown in full view of the audience on a stage, simulating the actual conditions of a radio broadcast; or, (2) in darkness, with its cast behind the scenes, and the result piped through a public address system loudspeaker into an auditorium, as a kind of radio show. In some ways the latter method is preferable, since every scene was originally conceived in terms of sound alone. However, such a performance might lack audience interest, and I have therefore made additions to the original script, indicated by new stage directions in brackets ([ ]) for visual performance. The director may choose the original radio version, or the version with the bracketed additions, depending on the conditions under which he happens to be working.

Dramatists Play Service reminds all persons that it cannot authorize the use of THE HITCH-HIKER for *actual radio broadcasting*. All groups, amateur or professional, interested in using the play over the radio, must secure permission from the William Morris Agency, 1350 Avenue of the Americas, New York, N. Y. 10019.

However, the Play Service is the only agent who can permit production of this play *by nonprofessionals, on the stage,* either without lights or *as though* in an actual broadcasting studio. While the Service cannot authorize actual radio broadcasting, it will allow a broadcast over a public address system, when it is strictly confined to the building where the production takes place. For necessary authorization for such presentations write Dramatists Play Service, 440 Park Avenue South, New York, N. Y. 10016.

In any case, THE HITCH-HIKER requires no scenery or props for its presentation, only a bare stage, a semicircle of chairs, where the actors wait for their cues, a microphone (real or not, depending on whether PA is used), one or two record-players, manual sound-effects (i.e. actual sounds produced by the crew, or sound records, or both), and a piano or musical records. The actors do not need to memorize their lines. They may read from scripts. Acting—that is in the stage sense, involving movement and gestures—is unnecessary. In this play, the microphone, not the live audience, should always be the focal point of projection. It is an ear for listening, not an eye for seeing.

If the performance is to be in darkness, and a public address system microphone used, it should be treated, like the radio microphone, as an instrument sensitive to every nuance of sound. The placement of sound-effects and music in relation to the actors must be studied, that they mutually complement each other. If one remembers that, lacking scenery of any kind in radio, the sound effects and the musical theme must take their places to create the illusion of reality, the importance of correct sound-levels in either type of performance will be understood.

In the Orson Welles production, recordings were used for nearly all the sound-effects indicated, and in the case of the telephone sequence, a real telephone with a coin-drop was brought in. This equipment may not be available, but with an ingenious sound-crew, substitutes for the smaller noises can be made. The main principle to be followed is that nothing sounds so real as the real thing, as in the case of door-slams, footsteps, slaps, bells, etc. The sound effect of the car motor and the approach of the train may be secured on records, which the

Service can furnish, as follows: An automobile starting up and running continuously (No. 5041); a passenger train, passing at high speed, with a whistle (No. 5049). Price, $3.75 each, packing and postage charges included.

Music is a most important requirement in this play. It would be ideal if one could find, as one so often can, a talented young pianist, able to devise a series of chords of a dark shuddery nature, and one theme of dreary melody and hollow harmony. Two or three cues of this type are sufficient, for once set, they may be repeated over and over again. The very monotony of the repetition adds to the eeriness, and produces more readily than fresh themes or chords an atmosphere of nightmare.

If such a pianist cannot be found, I suggest the use of a musical record. The selection is optional, depending on the taste of the director, and conforming to the type of themes I have suggested in the script. Here again, the repetition of one or two themes, rather than many, is most effective.

The main thing to remember in performing THE HITCH-HIKER is that we are relating a ghost story—one that takes place on a bare stage, and in the midst of much technical manipulation, but which, in spite of everything, must come off as a thing unearthly. How well it does that will depend on many things—on the sincerity, of course, and ability of the main actor—also on the efficiency and foresight of the director, and above all on the cooperation of cast and crew. Even a small slip can turn horror into comedy—which is one reason why good ghost stories are so rare, even on the professional stage. However, Orson Welles and his group of Mercury Players made of this script a haunting study of the supernatural, which can still raise hackles along my own spine—and given a touch of his dramatic flair, and a dash of his Mercury Players' spirit, I hope and believe it may create something of the same effect on others. I offer the present text for study and use by producing groups who may wish to present it by means of other techniques than that for which I originally wrote it.

LUCILLE FLETCHER

CAST

Ronald Adams
Mrs. Adams
The Hitch-Hiker
Filling Station Attendant
Road Stand Proprietor
Road Stand Proprietor's Wife
Girl Hitch-Hiker
Local Gallup Operator
Long Distance Operator
New York Operator
Albuquerque Operator
Mrs. Whitney

TECHNICAL

Director
Music
Sound Recordings
Manual Recordings One
Manual Recordings Two

The Hitch-Hiker

MUSIC: *Opening chords, dark and ominous. A piano may be used, or a brief passage from some orchestral record. The selection will depend on the* DIRECTOR'S *individual taste, but its major effect should consist of a strong, terrifying opening, followed by a kind of monotonous eeriness. The eerie part of the music continues throughout following speech, but faded down so that the words are audible.*

[SCENE: *As curtains part, we see a stage set up for a radio broadcast. Central microphone, at which* RONALD ADAMS *is standing. A semicircle of chairs, rear, on which entire cast is seated. Sound-effects and music grouped wherever their level will complement and bolster the voice, but not overbalance it. Relative sound-levels are vitally important in this production, and should be carefully studied for maximum effectiveness.*]

RONALD ADAMS. I am in an auto camp on Route Sixty-six just west of Gallup, New Mexico. If I tell it, perhaps it will help me. It will keep me from going mad. But I must tell this quickly. I am not mad now. I feel perfectly well, except that I am running a slight temperature. My name is Ronald Adams. I am thirty-six years of age, unmarried, tall, dark, with a black mustache. I drive a Buick, license number 6Y-175-189. I was born in Brooklyn. All this I know. I know that I am at this moment perfectly sane. That it is not me who has gone mad—but something else—something utterly beyond my control. But I must speak quickly. At any moment the link may break. This may be the last thing I ever tell on earth . . . the last night I ever see the stars . . . (*Pause. Music fades out.*) [SCENE: MRS. ADAMS *rises from chair, rear, and comes forward to microphone.*] Six days ago I left Brooklyn, to drive to California.

MRS. ADAMS. Good-bye, son. Good luck to you, my boy.

ADAMS. Good-bye, Mother. Here—give me a kiss, and then I'll go.
MRS. A. I'll come out with you to the car.
ADAMS. No. It's raining. Stay here at the door. Hey—what's this? Tears? I thought you promised me you wouldn't cry?
MRS. A. I know, dear. I'm sorry. But I—do hate to see you go.
ADAMS. I'll be back. I'll only be on the Coast three months.
MRS. A. Oh—it isn't that. It's just—the trip. Ronald—I wish you weren't driving.
ADAMS. Oh, Mother. There you go again. People do it every day.
MRS. A. I know. But you'll be careful, won't you? Promise me you'll be extra careful. Don't fall asleep—or drive fast—or pick up any strangers on the road.
ADAMS. Gosh—no. You'd think I was still seventeen to hear you talk.
MRS. A. And wire me as soon as you get to Hollywood, won't you, son?
ADAMS. Of course I will. Now, don't you worry. There isn't anything going to happen. It's just eight days of perfectly simple driving on smooth civilized roads. (MANUAL SOUND: *Slam of car door.* SOUND RECORDING: *Car starts. Sound of car motor running.*) With a hot dog or a hamburger stand every ten miles. . . . (*He chuckles slightly.*) (SOUND RECORDING: *Automobile in motion full.*) (*Calling.*) G'bye, Mom —— [SCENE: MRS. ADAMS *leaves microphone, returning to row of chairs at rear stage.*] (*Sound recording of automobile continues behind following.*) I was in excellent spirits. The drive ahead of me, even the loneliness, seemed like a lark. But I reckoned—without—*him.* (MUSIC: *Dark opening chords, followed by theme of eerie quality. Continue faded down as before, mingling with sound of car motor running.*) Crossing Brooklyn Bridge that morning in the rain, I saw a man leaning against the cables. He seemed to be waiting for a lift. There were spots of fresh rain on his shoulders. He was carrying a cheap overnight bag in one hand. He was thin, nondescript, with a cap pulled down over his eyes. . . . (*Music fades out. Sound of auto continues.*) I would have forgotten him completely, except that just an hour later, while crossing the Pulaski Skyway over the Jersey flats, I saw him again. At least he looked like the same

person. He was standing now, with one thumb pointing west. I couldn't figure out how he'd got there, but I thought probably one of those fast trucks had picked him up, beaten me to the Skyway, and let him off. I didn't stop for him. Then—late that night—I saw him again. (MUSIC: *Dark ominous chords, followed by eerie theme. Continue through following speech.*) It was on the new Pennsylvania Turnpike between Harrisburg and Pittsburgh. It's two hundred and sixty-five miles long with a very high speed limit. I was just slowing down for one of the tunnels, when I saw him—standing under an arc light by the side of the road. I could see him quite distinctly. The bag, the cap, even the spots of fresh rain spattered over his shoulders. (*Music stops.*) He hailed me this time.

HITCH-HIKER. (*Off-stage, through megaphone, hollowly.*) Hallooo. . . . (*Slightly closer.*) Hall . . . llooo. . . . (SOUND RECORDING: *Automobile running faster.*)

ADAMS. I stepped on the gas like a shot. That's lonely country through the Alleghenies, and I had no intention of stopping. Besides, the coincidence, or whatever it was, gave me the willies. (SOUND RECORDING: *Automobile out.*) I stopped at the next gas station. (MANUAL SOUND: *Nervous honking of horn.*) [SCENE: *The filling station attendant leaves chair and advances to microphone.*]

FILLING STATION MAN. Yes, sir.

ADAMS. Fill her up.

F. S. M. Certainly, sir. Check your oil, sir?

ADAMS. No, thanks. (MANUAL SOUND. *Clank of hose. Sound of insertion into gas tank. Tinkle of bell at regular intervals as though from filling station pump. This continues behind following conversation.*)

F. S. M. Nice night, isn't it?

ADAMS. Yes. It hasn't been raining here recently, has it?

F. S. M. Not a drop of rain all week.

ADAMS. H'm. I suppose that hasn't done your business any harm?

F. S. M. Oh—people drive through here all kinds of weather. Mostly business, you know. There aren't many pleasure cars out on the Turnpike this season of the year.

ADAMS. I suppose not. (*Casually.*) What about hitch-hikers?

F. S. M. Hitch-hikers—*here?* (MANUAL SOUND: *Tinkling bell stops. Sound of hose being detached.*)

ADAMS. What's the matter? Don't you ever see any?

F. S. M. Not much. If we did, it'd be a sight for sore eyes. (*Manual sound stops.*)

ADAMS. Why?

F. S. M. A guy'd be a fool who started out to hitch rides on this road. Look at it.

ADAMS. Then you've never seen anybody?

F. S. M. Nope. Mebbe they get the lift before the Turnpike starts —I mean—you know—just before the toll-house—but then it'd be a mighty long ride. Most cars wouldn't want to pick up a guy for that long a ride. This is pretty lonesome country here—mountains and woods. . . . You ain't seen anybody like that, have you?

ADAMS. No. (*Quickly.*) Oh, no, not at all. It was—just a technical question.

F. S. M. I see. Well—that'll be just a dollar forty-nine—with the tax. . . . [SCENE: FILLING STATION MAN *steps back from microphone, and returns to seat at rear of stage, as:*] (*Sound recording fades in automobile starting, motor hum. Continue through following:*)

ADAMS. The thing gradually passed from my mind, as sheer coincidence. I had a good night's sleep in Pittsburgh. I didn't think about the man all next day—until just outside of Zanesville, Ohio, I saw him again. (MUSIC: *Dark chords, followed by eeriness. Continue through following: Sound recording of auto motor fade down behind music and words, but continue quietly.*) It was a bright sunshiny afternoon. The peaceful Ohio fields, brown with the autumn stubble, lay dreaming in the golden light. I was driving slowly, drinking it in, when the road suddenly ended in a detour. In front of the barrier—*he* was standing. (SOUND RECORDING: *Motor hum fades out. Music continues.*) Let me explain about his appearance before I go on. I repeat. There was nothing sinister about him. He was as drab as a mud fence. Nor was his attitude menacing. He merely stood there, waiting, almost drooping a little, the cheap overnight bag in his hand. He looked as though he had been waiting there for hours. Then he looked up —— (*Music stops.*) He hailed me. He started to walk forward. . . .

HITCH-HIKER. (*Off-stage, through megaphone, hollowly.*) Hallooo. . . . Hallo . . . ooo. . . . (MANUAL SOUND: *Starter button. Sound of gears jamming. Through megaphone off-stage, closer.*) Hall-ooo. . . . (*Manual sound continues. Clash of gears. Dead starter.*)

ADAMS. (*Panicky.*) No—not just now. Sorry. . . .

HITCH-HIKER. (*Through megaphone off-stage.*) Going to Cal-i-fornia . . . a . . . ?

ADAMS. (*Panicky.*) No. Not today. The other way. Going to New York. Sorry. . . . (SOUND RECORDING: *Automobile starts noisily. Wildly.*) *Sorry* . . . ! (SOUND RECORDING: *Automobile hum continuing through following:*) After I got the car back onto the road again, I felt like a fool. Yet the thought of picking him up, of having him sit beside me was somehow unbearable. Yet at the same time, I felt more than ever, unspeakably alone. . . . (MUSIC: *Just the eerie section fades in above sound of automobile hum. It continues through following:*) Hour after hour went by. The fields, the towns, ticked off one by one. The light changed. I knew now that I was going to see him again. And though I dreaded the sight, I caught myself searching the side of the road, waiting for him to appear. . . . (*Music and sound recording out.* MANUAL RECORDING: *Horn honk two or three times. Pause. Nervous honk again.*) [SCENE: ROADSIDE STAND PROPRIETOR, *elderly rural type, comes forward to microphone.*] (MANUAL SOUND TWO: *Creak of squeaky door.*)

PROPRIETOR. (*Querulous, mountain voice.*) Yep? What is it? What do you want?

ADAMS. (*Breathless.*) You sell sandwiches and pop here, don't you?

PROPRIETOR. (*Cranky.*) Yep. We do. In the daytime. But we're closed up now for the night.

ADAMS. I know. But—I was wondering if you could possibly let me have a cup of coffee—black coffee.

PROPRIETOR. Not at this time of night, mister. My wife's the cook, and she's in bed. Mebbe further down the road, at the Honeysuckle Rest. (MANUAL SOUND: *Creak of door closing.*)

ADAMS. No—no—don't shut the door. Listen—just a minute ago, there was a man standing here—right beside this stand—a suspicious looking man. . . . [SCENE: PROPRIETOR'S WIFE *stands up, calling from chair at rear of stage, not moving forward.*]

PROPRIETOR'S WIFE. (*A quavery, whiny voice.*) Hen-ry? Who is it, Hen-ry?

PROPRIETOR. It's nobuddy, Mother. Just a feller thinks he wants a cup of coffee. Go back into bed. [SCENE: WIFE *stands beside chair, listening, then slowly begins creeping forward.*]

ADAMS. I don't mean to disturb you. But you see, I was driving along—when I just happened to look—and there he was. . . .

PROPRIETOR. What was he doing?

ADAMS. Nothing. He ran off—when I stopped the car.

PROPRIETOR. Then what of it? That's nothing to wake a man in the middle of his sleep about. . . .

WIFE. Mebbe he's been drinkin', Henry. . . . (*Calling.*)

PROPRIETOR. (*Sternly.*) Young man, I've got a good mind to turn you over to the sheriff ——

ADAMS. But—I ——

PROPRIETOR. You've been taking a nip, that's what you've been doing. And you haven't got anything better to do than to wake decent folk out of their hard-earned sleep. Get going. Go on.

WIFE. (*Calling.*) Jes' shet the door on him, Henry ——

ADAMS. But he looked as though he were going to rob you.

HENRY. I ain't got nothin' in this stand to lose. (MANUAL SOUND: *Door creaking closed.*) Now—on your way before I call out Sheriff Oakes. (*Door slams shut. Bolted.*) [SCENE: PROPRIETOR *and his wife return to their seats at rear of stage.*] (SOUND RECORDING: *Auto starting, motor running.*)

ADAMS. I got into the car again, and drove on slowly. I was beginning to hate the car. If I could have found a place to stop . . . to rest a little. But I was in the Ozark Mountains of Missouri now. The few resort places there were closed. Only an occasional log cabin, seemingly deserted, broke the monotony of the wild wooded landscape. I *had* seen him at that roadside stand. I knew I would see him again—perhaps at the next turn of the road. I knew that when I saw him next—I would run him down. (MUSIC: *Dark chords, followed by eerie melody.*) But I did not see him again until late next afternoon. (*Music continues eerily.* MANUAL SOUND: *The tinkling of signal bell at railroad crossroads. Continue through following:*) I had stopped the car at a sleepy little junction just across the border into Oklahoma . . . to let a train pass by—when he appeared across the tracks, leaning against a telephone pole. . . . (*Music and manual sound continuing. Very tense.*) It was a perfectly airless, dry day. The red clay of Oklahoma was baking under the south-western sun. Yet there were spots of fresh rain on his shoulders. . . . (*Music stops.*) I couldn't stand that. Without thinking, blindly, I started the car across the tracks. (SOUND RECORDING: *Distant, very faint cry of train whistle approaching. Manual sound of bell continuing.*) He didn't even look up at me. He was staring at the ground. I stepped on the gas hard, veering the wheel sharply toward him. (SOUND RECORDING: *Train whistle closer. Chugging of wheels fading in.*) I could hear the train in the distance now. But I didn't care. (MANUAL SOUND ONE *continues signal bell.* MANUAL SOUND TWO: *Jamming of gears. Clash of metal.*) Then—something went wrong with the car. (MANUAL SOUND TWO: *Gears jamming. Starter button dead.* SOUND RECORDING: *Train chugging up, louder.*) The train was coming closer. I could hear the cry of its whistle. (SOUND RECORDING: *Train chugging. Cry of whistle closer. (All this should be a cacophony of sound blended together, almost overriding* ADAMS' *voice, which tries to rise above it, almost hysterical with panic.*) Still he stood there. And now—I knew that he was beckoning—beckoning me to my death. . . . (SOUND RECORDING: *Full train chugging topped by wild cry of train whistle overpowering all other sound, full, then dying away slowly to silence. Music fades in with the eerie part of the theme. We hear this a second or two, then* ADAMS *says breathlessly, quietly:*) Well—I frustrated him that time. The starter worked at last. I managed to back up. But when the train passed, he was gone. I was all alone, in the hot dry afternoon. (*Music continuing.* SOUND RECORDING: *Fade in auto hum.*) After that, I knew I had to do something. I didn't know who this man was, or what he wanted of me. I only knew that from now on, I must not let myself be alone on the road for one moment. (*Music and sound recording of auto out.*) [SCENE: GIRL HITCH-HIKER *comes forward to microphone.*] (MANUAL RECORDING: *Honk of horn.*) Hello, there. Like a ride?

GIRL. What do you think? How far you going?

ADAMS. Where do you want to go?

GIRL. Amarillo, Texas. (MANUAL SOUND: *Car door opening.*)
ADAMS. I'll drive you there.
GIRL. Gee! (MANUAL SOUND: *Car door slams.* SOUND RECORDING: *Auto starting up, hum. It continues through following.*) Mind if I take off my shoes? My dogs are killing me.
ADAMS. Go right ahead.
GIRL. Gee, what a break this is. A swell car, a decent guy, and driving all the way to Amarillo. All I been getting so far is trucks.
ADAMS. Hitch-hike much?
GIRL. Sure. Only it's tough sometimes, in these great open spaces, to get the breaks.
ADAMS. I should think it would be. Though I'll bet if you get a good pick-up in a fast car, you can get to places faster than, say, another person in another car.
GIRL. I don't get you?
ADAMS. Well, take me, for instance. Suppose I'm driving across the country, say, at a nice steady clip of about forty-five miles an hour. Couldn't a girl like you, just standing beside the road, waiting for lifts, beat me to town after town—provided she got picked up every time in a car doing from sixty-five to seventy miles an hour?
GIRL. I dunno. What difference does it make?
ADAMS. Oh—no difference. It's just a—crazy idea I had sitting here in the car.
GIRL. (*Laughing.*) Imagine spending your time in a swell car, and thinking of things like that.
ADAMS. What would you do instead?
GIRL. (*Admiringly.*) What would I do? If I was a good-looking fellow like yourself? Why—I'd just *enjoy* myself—every minute of the time. I'd sit back and relax, and if I saw a good-looking girl along the side of the road . . . (*Sharply.*) Hey—look out! (SOUND RECORDING: *Auto hum continuing.*)
ADAMS. (*Breathlessly.*) Did you see him, too?
GIRL. See who?
ADAMS. That man. Standing beside the barbed-wire fence.
GIRL. I didn't see—nobody. There wasn't nothing but a bunch of steer—and the wire fence. What did you think you was doing? Trying to run into the barbed-wire fence? (SOUND RECORDING: *Auto motor continuing.*)

ADAMS. There was a man there, I tell you . . . a thin gray man, with an overnight bag in his hand. And I was trying to run him down.
GIRL. Run him down? You mean—kill him?
ADAMS. But—(*Desperately.*) you say you didn't see him back there? You're sure?
GIRL. (*Queerly.*) I didn't see a soul. And as far as I'm concerned, mister . . .
ADAMS. Watch for him the next time then. Keep watching. Keep your eyes peeled on the road. He'll turn up again—maybe any minute now. (*Excitedly.*) There! Look there. . . . (MANUAL RECORDING: *Car skidding. Screech. A crash of metal as of car going into barbed-wire fence.* GIRL *screams.* MANUAL RECORDING: *A bump.* MANUAL RECORDING TWO: *Sound of door handle of car turning.*)
GIRL. How does this door work? I—I'm gettin' out of here.
ADAMS. Did you see him that time?
GIRL. (*Sharply, choked.*) No. I didn't see him that time. And personally, mister, I don't expect never to see him. All I want to do is go on living—and I don't see how I will very long, driving with you.
ADAMS. I'm sorry. I—I don't know what came over me. (*Frightened.*) Please . . . don't go. . . .
GIRL. So if you'll excuse me, mister.
ADAMS. You can't go. Listen, how would you like to go to California? I'll drive you to California.
GIRL. Seeing pink elephants all the way? No, thanks. (MANUAL SOUND: *Door handle turning.*)
ADAMS. Listen. Please. For just one moment ——
GIRL. You know what I think you need, big boy? Not a girl friend. Just a dose of good sleep. There. I got it now. . . . (MANUAL SOUND: *Door opens. Slams. Metallic.*)
ADAMS. No. You can't go.
GIRL. (*Wildly.*) Leave your hands offa me, do you hear? Leave your —— (MANUAL SOUND: *Sharp slap.* 2ND MANUAL SOUND: *Footsteps over gravel, running. They die away. A pause.*)
ADAMS. She ran from me, as though I were a monster. A few minutes later, I saw a passing truck pick her up. I knew then that I was utterly alone. (MANUAL SOUND: *Imitation of low mooing of steer, or sound recording of same.*) I was in the

heart of the great Texas prairies. There wasn't a car on the road after the truck went by. I tried to figure out what to do, how to get hold of myself. If I could find a place to rest. Or even if I could sleep right there in the car for a few hours, along the side of the road. (MUSIC: *The eerie theme stealing in softly.*) I was getting my winter overcoat out of the back seat to use as a blanket, when I saw him coming toward me, emerging from the herd of moving steer. . . . (SOUND: *Mooing of steer, low. Out of it emerges voice of:*)

HITCH-HIKER. (*Hollowly off-stage through megaphone.*) Hall . . . ooo. . . . Hall . . . oo. . . . (SOUND RECORDING: *Auto starting. Auto hum steady up. Music continuing*)

ADAMS. Perhaps I should have spoken to him then, fought it out then and there. For now he began to be everywhere. Wherever I stopped, even for a moment—for gas, for oil, for a drink of pop, a cup of coffee, a sandwich—he was there. (*Music continuing. Auto sound continuing. More tense and rapid.*) I saw him standing outside the auto camp in Amarillo, that night, when I dared to slow down. He was sitting near the drinking fountain in a little camping spot just inside the border of New Mexico. . . . (*Music steady. Rapid, more breathless.*) He was waiting for me outside the Navajo Reservation where I stopped to check my tires. I saw him in Albuquerque, where I bought twenty gallons of gas. I was afraid now, afraid to stop. I began to drive faster and faster. I was in lunar landscape now—the great arid mesa country of New Mexico. I drove through it with the indifference of a fly crawling over the face of the moon. . . . (*Auto hum up. Music more and more eerie. More desperately.*) But now he didn't even wait for me to stop. Unless I drove at eighty-five miles an hour over those endless roads, he waited for me at every other mile. I would see his figure, shadowless, flitting before me, still in its same attitude, over the cold lifeless ground, flitting over dried-up rivers, over broken stones cast up by old glacial upheavals, flitting in the pure and cloudless air. . . . (*Music reaches eerie climax. Stops. Sound recording of auto hum stops. A low voice in the silence.*) I was beside myself when I finally reached Gallup, New Mexico, this morning. There is an auto camp here—cold, almost deserted at this time of year. I went inside and asked if there was a telephone. . . . (MANUAL RECORDING:

Sound of footsteps on wood, heavy, echoing.) I had the feeling that if only I could speak to someone familiar, someone I loved, I could pull myself together. [SCENE: FIRST OPERATOR *rises, comes forward to microphone.*] (MANUAL SOUND: *Nickel put into phone.*)

OPERATOR. Number, please?

ADAMS. Long distance.

OPERATOR. Thank you. [SCENE: LONG DISTANCE OPERATOR *comes forward to microphone.*] (MANUAL SOUND: *Return of nickel. Buzz.*)

LONG DISTANCE. This is Long Distance.

ADAMS. I'd like to put in a call to my home in Brooklyn, New York. I'm Ronald Adams. The number is Beechwood 2-0828.

LONG DISTANCE. Thank you. What is your number? [*A mechanical tone.*]

ADAMS. My number . . . 312. [SCENE: THIRD OPERATOR *rises from chair, remaining at rear stage.*] (MANUAL SOUND: *A buzz.*)

3RD OPERATOR. (*From distance.*) Albuquerque.

LONG DISTANCE OPERATOR. New York for Gallup. [SCENE: FOURTH OPERATOR *rises, stands beside chair at rear stage.*]

4TH OPERATOR. New York.

LONG DISTANCE. Gallup, New Mexico, calling Beechwood 2-0828. [SCENE: FOURTH OPERATOR *steps back a little distance from microphone during following.*]

ADAMS. I had read somewhere that love could banish demons. It was the middle of the morning. I knew Mother would be home. I pictured her tall, white-haired, in her crisp house dress, going about her tasks. It would be enough, I thought, merely to hear the even calmness of her voice.

LONG DISTANCE. Will you please deposit three dollars and eighty-five cents for the first three minutes. When you have deposited a dollar and a half will you wait until I have collected the money? [SCENE: *Other three* OPERATORS *sit down.*] (MANUAL SOUND: *Clunk of six quarters as through telephone.*) All right, deposit another dollar and a half. (MANUAL SOUND: *Clunk of six quarters as through telephone.*) Will you please deposit the remaining eighty-five cents? (SOUND: *Clunk of three quarters and one dime as through telephone.*) Ready with Brooklyn—go ahead, please. [SCENE: LONG DISTANCE *steps back little farther toward rear, as* MRS. WHITNEY *comes forward to* C. *microphone.*]

ADAMS. Hello.

MRS. WHITNEY. Mrs. Adams' residence.

ADAMS. Hello. Hello—Mother?

MRS. WHITNEY. (*Very flat and proper.*) This is Mrs. Adams' residence. Who is it you wished to speak to, please? [*N. B. If this script is to be done with invisible actors, it would be wise in the telephone sequences to attempt to reproduce the sound of the voices* ADAMS *hears, as much like telephone voices as possible. This could be done by the use of another microphone and a filter to eliminate the lower tones. If the* OPERATORS *and* MRS. WHITNEY *use such a microphone, it should be isolated in the studio, by a screen. If this is not feasible, then some other attempt should be made to give the effect of distance, remoteness, and thinness. It could be achieved in a visual performance merely by placing the* OPERATORS *and* MRS. WHITNEY *at different distances from microphone. In other words,* ADAMS' *position should be dominant, and his voice close—theirs, far off, and maddeningly faint.*]

ADAMS. Why—who's this?

MRS. WHITNEY. This is Mrs. Whitney.

ADAMS. Mrs. Whitney? I don't know any Mrs. Whitney. Is this Beechwood 2-0828?

MRS. WHITNEY. Yes.

ADAMS. Where's my mother? Where's Mrs. Adams?

MRS. WHITNEY. Mrs. Adams is not at home. She is still in the hospital.

ADAMS. The hospital?

MRS. WHITNEY. Yes. Who is this calling, please? Is it a member of the family?

ADAMS. What's she in the hospital for?

MRS. WHITNEY. She's been prostrated for five days. Nervous breakdown. But who is this calling?

ADAMS. Nervous breakdown? But—my mother was never nervous.

MRS. WHITNEY. It's all taken place since the death of her oldest son, Ronald.

ADAMS. Death of her oldest son, Ronald . . . ? Hey—what is this? What number is this?

MRS. WHITNEY. This is Beechwood 2-0828. It's all been very sudden. He was killed just six days ago in an automobile accident on the Brooklyn Bridge. [SCENE: LONG DISTANCE OPERATOR *comes forward.*]

LONG DISTANCE. Your three minutes are up, sir. (*Pause.*) Your three minutes are up, sir. . . . [SCENE: LONG DISTANCE OPERATOR *and* MRS. WHITNEY *back away, as* ADAMS *stands there.*] Sir—your three minutes are up. . . . [SCENE: LONG DISTANCE OPERATOR *and* MRS. WHITNEY *sit down.*] Your three minutes are up, sir. . . . (*Softly. A pause.* MUSIC: *Fade in eerie theme softly.*)

ADAMS. (*A strange voice.*) And so, I am sitting here in this deserted auto camp in Gallup, New Mexico. I am trying to think. I am trying to get hold of myself. Otherwise I shall go mad. . . . Outside it is night—the vast, soulless night of New Mexico. A million stars are in the sky. Ahead of me stretch a thousand miles of empty mesa, mountains, prairies, desert. Somewhere, among them, he is waiting for me. . . . [SCENE: *He turns slowly from microphone, looking off-stage, in direction of* HITCH-HIKER's *voice.*] Somewhere I shall know who he is—and who . . . I am. . . . (*Music continues to an eerie climax.*) [SCENE: ADAMS *walks slowly away from microphone, and off stage, as CURTAIN FALLS.*]

THE END

NEW PLAYS

★ **CLYBOURNE PARK by Bruce Norris.** WINNER OF THE 2011 PULITZER PRIZE AND 2012 TONY AWARD. Act One takes place in 1959 as community leaders try to stop the sale of a home to a black family. Act Two is set in the same house in the present day as the now predominantly African-American neighborhood battles to hold its ground. "Vital, sharp-witted and ferociously smart." *–NY Times.* "A theatrical treasure…Indisputably, uproariously funny." *–Entertainment Weekly.* [4M, 3W] ISBN: 978-0-8222-2697-0

★ **WATER BY THE SPOONFUL by Quiara Alegría Hudes.** WINNER OF THE 2012 PULITZER PRIZE. A Puerto Rican veteran is surrounded by the North Philadelphia demons he tried to escape in the service. "This is a very funny, warm, and yes uplifting play." *–Hartford Courant.* "The play is a combination poem, prayer and app on how to cope in an age of uncertainty, speed and chaos." *–Variety.* [4M, 3W] ISBN: 978-0-8222-2716-8

★ **RED by John Logan.** WINNER OF THE 2010 TONY AWARD. Mark Rothko has just landed the biggest commission in the history of modern art. But when his young assistant, Ken, gains the confidence to challenge him, Rothko faces the agonizing possibility that his crowning achievement could also become his undoing. "Intense and exciting." *–NY Times.* "Smart, eloquent entertainment." *–New Yorker.* [2M] ISBN: 978-0-8222-2483-9

★ **VENUS IN FUR by David Ives.** Thomas, a beleaguered playwright/director, is desperate to find an actress to play Vanda, the female lead in his adaptation of the classic sadomasochistic tale *Venus in Fur.* "Ninety minutes of good, kinky fun." *–NY Times.* "A fast-paced journey into one man's entrapment by a clever, vengeful female." *–Associated Press.* [1M, 1W] ISBN: 978-0-8222-2603-1

★ **OTHER DESERT CITIES by Jon Robin Baitz.** Brooke returns home to Palm Springs after a six-year absence and announces that she is about to publish a memoir dredging up a pivotal and tragic event in the family's history—a wound they don't want reopened. "Leaves you feeling both moved and gratifyingly sated." *–NY Times.* "A genuine pleasure." *–NY Post.* [2M, 3W] ISBN: 978-0-8222-2605-5

★ **TRIBES by Nina Raine.** Billy was born deaf into a hearing family and adapts brilliantly to his family's unconventional ways, but it's not until he meets Sylvia, a young woman on the brink of deafness, that he finally understands what it means to be understood. "A smart, lively play." *–NY Times.* "[A] bright and boldly provocative drama." *–Associated Press.* [3M, 2W] ISBN: 978-0-8222-2751-9